WORDPRESS

PLUGINS

The 672 Best Free WordPress Plugins for
Developing Amazing and Profitable Websites

~2019 Edition~

Eliot Tennant

*****

Remember to back up your website/database regularly, and before installing any plugins as a best practice and security precaution.

Links are clickable in the e-book. The e-book is free of charge with the purchase of the paperback edition.

Contents

INTRODUCTION

In 2009, I hired a website designer to help me with a blog I was starting. I didn't have a clue about how to create a website, so I needed support. After the creation of three sample sites and mounting expenses, I began to learn how to make websites. The designer used WordPress, so I started to learn more about it. The ability to create efficient websites quickly is an extremely important technical, business, and marketing skill to possess. Knowing how to design and develop a functional website provides endless self-employment, entrepreneurial, and side hustle opportunities.

Ten years later, I've created many websites—some good and some bad—and I've enjoyed evolving with WordPress. It's easy to use, amazingly powerful, and practical. I still don't know or need to know how to code because thousands of WordPress themes and plugins take care of site development, management, improvement, and technicalities.

WordPress is a free open-source website software application and content management system (CMS). There are thousands of free and paid themes and plugins available for site development. A theme is a website template and framework that can be customized by its user. A plugin extends the functionality of a website, for example, a search engine optimization (SEO) plugin enables a user to easily add SEO text/details to posts and pages.

WordPress powers roughly 30 percent of all websites and leads the way in content management systems with a market share of around 60 percent. You can visit Wikipedia for more details.

With 54,000 plus plugins, there are many to choose from and everyone has their favorites. I've searched high and low and page after page to bring you the best free plugins in over thirty categories. Many articles describe the "best," "must-have," and "top" plugins, but none of them are as comprehensive as my list. This book is your ultimate reference guide. This list of 672 plugins represents roughly 1.24 percent of all plugins listed on WordPress.org.

To your success!

Eliot Tennant, WordPress Enthusiast

WORDPRESS.ORG VS. WORDPRESS.COM

There can be some confusion between WordPress.org and WordPress.com, so let's understand their differences.

WordPress.org

WordPress.org provides free open-source software to run a website, blog, or app. It acts as an information repository for all things WordPress. You will find plenty of information and resources regarding themes, plugins, documentation, and support.

In tandem with the free open-source software, you'll need hosting to run your site. WordPress.org recommends Bluehost, DreamHost, and SiteGround for hosting (I'm with SiteGround). However, thousands of hosting companies/providers exist. Web hosting cost around seven to ten dollars a month depending on the provider and plan. To purchase and renew a domain name costs ten to fifteen dollars annually, for example, www.yourdomain.com. Setting up WordPress through a hosting company is achieved through an efficient one-click installation process that takes a few minutes. If you need affordable hosting or would like to companies, click here or visit www.digitalfodder.com/cheap-web-hosting-for-wordpress/

The open-source environment of WordPress.org attracts thousands of developers who create free and paid themes and plugins for everyone to use, which yields a lot of selection. User support for free themes/plugins can be hit or miss depending on the developer. Users can also purchase themes and plugins, which usually come with more features and support. I've purchased plugins from Elegant Themes and Thrive Themes.

WordPress.com

WordPress.com offers WordPress software, hosting, support, themes, and plugins all in one place. It's a one-stop-shop for websites managed by Automattic—a website development company. The founder of Automattic, Matt Mullenweg, is also the founder of the WordPress software and foundation that runs WordPress.org.

WordPress.com controls the themes and plugins users can access on their personal and premium plans ($48 and $96 billed yearly). Only on the WordPress.com business plan can users add themes and plugins at their discretion ($300 charged annually). A free domain name for one year is included with all paid plans.

WordPress.com offers nearly 300 free and paid themes, which pales in comparison to the thousands of themes available on WordPress.org. Their assortment of themes and plugins vary and satisfies most customers. Jetpack is their main plugin. It's an all-in-one plugin that consists of multiple functions such as backup, performance, security, SEO, and more. It's also available through WordPress.org. Automattic manages technical issues, and they provide excellent customer support.

You can get a free website at WordPress.com if you don't mind using an address like yourname.wordpress.com. However, you aren't likely to show up in search engine results or be taken seriously by others.

Which Is Better?

WordPress.com is ideal for people who want convenience, support, and don't mind fewer theme and plugin options (excluding the business plan). WordPress.org is ideal for individuals who want greater control and options for a hands-on approach. WooCommerce, for e-commerce functionality, is available on both platforms. WordPress.com has a comparison breakdown on their site.
WordPress.org and WordPress.com are both excellent solutions, so you can't go wrong with either. Also, they are more versatile and user-friendly than Squarespace, Weebly, and Wix among others.

Up to 87% off WordPress Hosting

https://www.digitalfodder.com/cheap-web-hosting-for-wordpress/

WordPress Communities

Thousands of WordPress users flock to WordPress.org for support. However, support and social interactions are available on other websites and face-to-face.

Facebook

There are many WordPress themed Facebook groups. Some groups allow members to discuss all things WordPress compared with other groups that focus on specific topics. For example, a group that discusses plugins only. To avoid getting banned, it's critical to understand the group's rules and guidelines before posting or commenting.

To find WordPress groups on Facebook, type "WordPress" in the Facebook search bar then select the "Groups" tab. See this post for the fifteen best Facebook groups for WordPress users.

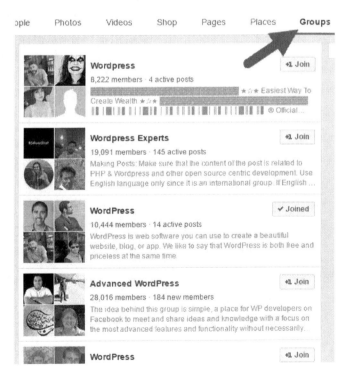

LinkedIn

Groups have never LinkedIn's strong suite, but many WordPress groups exist.

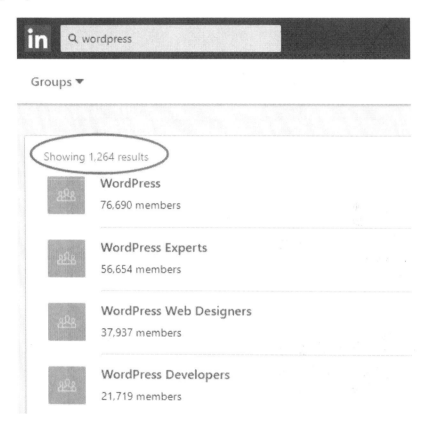

WordCamp

WordCamps are casual, locally-organized conferences covering WordPress. WordCamps include sessions on how to optimize WordPress, advanced techniques, security, and more. WordCamps are attended by bloggers, developers, website designers, and consultants. Events combine scheduled programming with conference sessions and other activities. To get an idea of the WordCamp experience, check out the WordCamp channel on WordPress.tv.

GUTEN-WHAT?

"Gutenberg" is the name of the project to create a new post and page editing experience in WordPress. "Blocks" are the main feature of Gutenberg and are meant to replace shortcodes, embeds, widgets, post formats, custom post types, theme options, meta-boxes, and other formatting elements. Gutenberg was released in December 2018.

Meet your new best friends, Blocks

Blocks are a great new tool for building engaging content. With blocks, you can insert, rearrange, and style multimedia content with very little technical knowledge. Instead of using custom code, you can add a block and focus on your content.

Why blocks? I suspect the folks at WordPress noticed the growing popularity of page builders that use elements (blocks) from companies like Elegant Themes (Divi), Thrive Themes (Thrive Architect), and Elementor. So, they decided to jump on the bandwagon.

Perhaps it's a reluctance to change, but many WordPress users have not embraced Gutenberg. The Gutenberg plugin has an abysmal rating of two out of five stars. To make users happy, WordPress created the Classic Editor plugin. It restores the previous "classic" WordPress editor and the "Edit Post" screen. I'm not sold on Gutenberg and prefer the classic editor.

A LITTLE CSS GOES ALONG WAY

For many years, I would use a theme and take the good with the bad. If I disliked an attribute, I would leave it. Last year, I changed my approach by learning about CSS. My desire to learn CSS began when I wanted to change the font size of my menu's text. I searched for a how-to video and learned from Greg Narayan about how to make the change. (I highly recommend watching his <u>video</u>.)

CSS, or Cascading Style Sheets, is a presentation language created to style the appearance of content, for example, background color, font-size, font-family, and color. CSS describes how HTML elements should be displayed. HTML, or Hypertext Markup Language, gives content structure and meaning by defining page contents, for example, headings, paragraphs, and images.

HTML = Structure

CSS = Decoration & Design

CSS might be the answer to your problems. Basic CSS instructions are easy to implement and can improve the design of your site. Since I don't have a background in coding, I typically research what CSS instructions I must use. That's one of the many benefits of search engines.

What I've Been Doing

Using the Google Chrome browser, I navigate to the page/style attribute I want to change, right click, choose "Inspect," and search for the element, for example, "font-family."

In a second browser window, I'll navigate to Appearance > Customize > Additional CSS (on the WordPress dashboard). That's where I'll input my CSS instructors.

```
 3 }
 4 .main-navigation ul {
 5 font-size: 1.5rem;
 6 }
 7 .main-navigation a {
 8     color: #ffffff;
 9 }
10 .home .main-navigation a {
11     color: #ffffff;
12 }
13 .widget-area {
14     font-size: 1.4rem;
15 }
16 * {font-family:Helvetica}
17 .post-navigation { display:
   none; }
18 .widget-area aside {
19 height: 250px
20 }
```

If the format/code of your instruction is incorrect, WordPress will warn you in which case you **shouldn't proceed** until the warning goes away.

There are 2 errors which must be fixed before you can save.

☐ Update anyway, even though it might break your site?

```
 4 .main-navigation ul {
 5 font-size: 1.5rem;
 6 }
 7 .main-navigation a {
 8     color: #ffffff;
 9 }
10 .home .main-navigation a {
11     color: #ffffff;
12 }
13 .widget-area {
14     font-size: 1.4rem;
15 }
16 * {font-family:Helvetica}
17 .post-navigation { display:
```
❌ 24 {}

CSS Plugins

A few free CSS plugins are available and eliminate the need to enter codes manually. You'll find them in the CSS Plugin category. CSS Hero is a premium CSS plugin that's worth reviewing.

How to Secure Your Site

WordPress software is robust. However, it's vulnerable to attacks if security measures aren't taken. The degree of security you need depends on the purpose of your site, for example, a blog can afford fewer security efforts than an e-commerce site that maintains customer data. Still, all sites need protection to thwart hackers and bad actors who seek to compromise websites.

In this post, SiteGround, a web hosting company, highlights five critical activities:

- Keep your WordPress site and plugins up-to-date
- Protect your WordPress admin area
- Don't use the "admin" username
- Use strong passwords
- Ensure your computer is free of viruses and malware

CodeinWP offers 23 security ideas, but you don't have to implement all of them; only those that apply to your situation. Separately, I recommend the following measures:

- Install a top-rated security plugin and review its settings. I use Wordfence.
- Change your login URL from yoursite.com/wp-login to yoursite.com/(whatever you want). The easiest way to achieve that is with the WPS Hide Login plugin.
- Encrypt your site. Encrypting your site is easy and free with Let's Encrypt. This article discusses the process in detail.

- Remove deactivated plugins.

HOW TO SPEED UP YOUR SITE

The speed at which a site's pages load is critical to a user's experience. Page speed is also important to Google, which states,

People want to be able to find answers to their questions as fast as possible — studies show that people really care about the speed of a page. Although speed has been used in ranking for some time, that signal was focused on desktop searches. Today we're announcing that starting in July 2018, page speed will be a ranking factor for mobile searches.

I've been obsessed with page speed for a couple of years, and my website is the fastest it's ever been. My desktop score is a perfect 100 while my mobile score fluctuates between 75 to 85. I could remove things like opt-in forms to achieve a higher mobile score, but a lower score is a tradeoff I'm willing to accept to grow my email list.

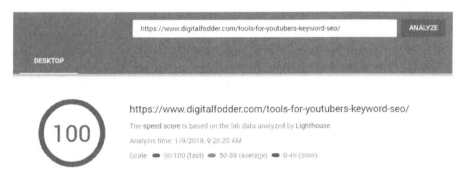

Three Steps to Increase Your Page Speed

1. Get Your Score

Google's PageSpeed Insights is undoubtedly the tool of choice for page speed scoring and analysis. It analyzes the content of a web page, then generates suggestions to make that page faster. Other scoring sites and tools include:

- Google Mobile-Friendly   Test (https://search.google.com/test/mobile-friendly)
- GTmetrix (gtmetrix.com)
- Pingdom (tools.pingdom.com)
- Website Grader (website.grader.com)

Most page speed tools borrow at least a part of their assessment methodology from PageSpeed Insights. Still, it's beneficial to get different insights regarding performance.

2. Understand Your Problem Areas

PageSpeed Insights will highlight "opportunities" to make your site faster. Opportunities feature drop-down menus to learn more.

Common opportunities/problems pertain to:

- Remove render-blocking resources
- Reduce image sizes
- Minify the HTML output
- Minify JavaScript files
- Minify CSS files
- Remove query strings from static resources
- Use GZIP compression

- Use Browser caching
- Use expiry headers
- Reduce HTTP requests

3. Install Plugins to Speed up Your Site

Cache, optimization, and performance plugins are listed in this book. I recommend WP Fastest Cache and WP Super Cache. WP-Optimize is an excellent plugin to maintain an efficient database. Autoptimize is a highly rated performance plugin that can solve many PageSpeed opportunities. Smush Image Compression and Optimization is a first-rate plugin to optimize image files. Finally, BJ Lazy Load is a good option if your cache plugin doesn't include a lazy load option.

As you experiment with plugins, review your site to ensure everything remains functional. For example, after selecting a couple of performance options with one plugin, the "X" on my cookie notice popup didn't work. (It probably didn't work after choosing a minify option of some sort). Secondly, review and adjust a plugin's settings to optimize it. Many users never check or change settings, which could produce missed opportunities.

Other Considerations

Your WordPress theme impacts its speed and performance. When a theme is complex or ill designed, it will slow load times. Use a theme that is efficient, responsive, and mobile-friendly.

Web hosting companies do not perform the same. Since moving from DreamHost to SiteGround, my page speeds have increased. I frequently had issues with DreamHost including my site going offline for several hours and inefficient customer support. DreamHost appears to be focused on their website's appearance whereas SiteGround is concerned with server performance. SiteGround routinely ranks well by reviewers. They also offer an all-in-one cache/performance plugin, which is how I achieved my high scores. At first glance, the SG Optimizer plugin has a low rating. Many negative reviews state the plugin doesn't work. The plugin won't work for a non-SiteGround customer because the user needs a license key—provided by SiteGround—to activate the plugin. When you factor out "not working" and reviews older than one year, the plugin scores well. You might also consider A2 Hosting and InMotion Hosting for web hosting.

I occasionally come across websites that feature multiple marketing and communication interrupters including scroll mats, notification bars, opt-in forms, web push notifications, cookie notices, and so forth. You can have various interrupters, but they need to be well planned, timed, and executed so that they don't appear all at once or on every page. Also, your goal shouldn't be to bombard your visitors.

Up to 87% off WordPress Hosting

https://www.digitalfodder.com/cheap-web-hosting-for-wordpress/

EMAIL MARKETING PLUGINS VS. STANDALONE SOFTWARE

WordPress is a website software application; not an email marketing service. However, that hasn't stopped a handful of developers from creating email marketing and newsletter plugins.

In the infancy of my online marketing experience, I used a WordPress email plugin. I disliked the interface and results I got. I've since used MailChimp, AWeber, and currently use MailerLite.

I don't recommend using an email marketing plugin for the following reasons:

1. Email marketing plugins lag in features and innovation compared to email marketing services. For example, MailerLite has an auto resend feature that automatically sends a second email to subscribers who didn't open the first one.
2. Plugins and subscribers are a hassle to transfer from one site to another. Email marketing services don't suffer from

transportability issues because they're independent of WordPress.

3. Plugins don't offer significant price savings compared to MailerLite and MailChimp.
4. Plugins don't integrate with leading software and WordPress companies such as Shopify, Leadpages, HubSpot, Elegant Themes, and Thrive Themes.
5. Plugin sites don't offer real-time or live chat support.
6. Most top online marketers and influencers don't promote, use, or recommend email marketing plugins. (That should tell you something.)
7. Email marketing plugins typically don't have affiliate programs, which sucks for affiliate marketers.

Many email marketing providers have free plans like plugin companies. In this post, I discuss MailChimp alternatives and free email marketing services.

THE TRUTH ABOUT WORDPRESS SEO PLUGINS

Search engine optimization (SEO) is the process of influencing the online visibility of a website or web page in a search engine's unpaid results—often referred to as "natural," "organic," or "earned" results. In 2018, SEO strategies helped me to increase my traffic by 6x. Yes, 6x! The image below represents my traffic growth, which started to decline upon rebranding my domain to digitalfodder.com (a decline in traffic is typical).

chadtennant.com Traffic Statistics

Find similar sites to chadtennant.com

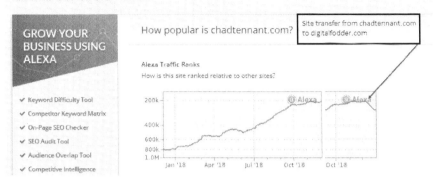

Many studies highlight the importance of being on the first page of search results. Call it convenience or laziness, most searchers limit their click throughs to page one results. According to one study, "On average, 71.33% of searches result in a page one organic click. Page two and three get only 5.59% of the clicks. On the first page alone, the first five results account for 67.60% of all the clicks and the results from 6 to 10 account for only 3.73%."

There are many WordPress SEO plugins, and I use the All in One SEO Pack. However, SEO plugins are **useless** without an understanding of SEO. Learning about SEO and implementing the best practices won't guarantee top rankings. Nevertheless, it will provide you with strategic advantages and allow you to pick your search rankings battles more wisely. For example, I've chosen not to write about specific topics because those posts probably wouldn't rank well (given the competition). You should learn about SEO if you:

- Create content regularly
- Own or manage a website or blog
- Have a desire to expand your digital marketing strategies
- Conduct online marketing activities such as affiliate, content, social media, and video marketing
- Generate revenue on online marketplaces, for example, Amazon, eBay, Fiverr, and Upwork

Critical Search Engine Ranking Factors

Since this is a book about WordPress, I'm not going to write a novel on SEO. Of the 200 or so ranking factors, I prioritize these five:

1. Highly quality, optimized posts of at least 1,000 words
2. Page title
3. Page description
4. Page URL
5. Page speed

My site uses Secure Sockets Layer (SSL) for security, which Google takes into consideration.

Courses, Tutorials, and Resources

SEO educational content is everywhere you look and often free. Therefore, there's no need to pay to learn about SEO. A few years ago, I took an SEO course on Coursera. Coursera has a handful of SEO courses and a specialization. You can also explore:

- Search Engine Optimization (SEO) Starter Guide by Google
- A Complete Guide to SEO: What You Need to Know by Search Engine Journal
- SEO Learning Center by Moz
- A Complete Guide to SEO: What You Need to Know by HubSpot
- The Beginner's Guide to E-commerce SEO by Shopify

YouTube has thousands of videos about SEO. Also, Skillshare, Udacity, and Udemy are popular e-learning platforms that have SEO courses.

FREE AND PAID PLUGINS AND THEMES

With thousands of free plugins and themes available, why would anyone pay for either? Most of the time free plugins/themes will suffice, but sometimes they won't. Sometimes "free" can only take you so far. You may want features such as analytics, customer support, and customization, which free plugins often lack. For example, if growing your email list is a priority, you'll want a robust opt-in form plugin to help you convert. While there are several free and excellent popup plugins, their features are limited. I wasn't content after trying a couple of free plugins, so I purchased Bloom by Elegant Themes. My conversion rates and results are fantastic.

Many premium plugins and themes cost $20 to $100. When considering what free and paid plugins/themes to use, I recommend taking the following steps:

1. Before beginning your search for a plugin or theme, put on your project management hat and **define your requirements**. Consider and predetermine your objectives, needs, and priorities for your website. Your thoughts and ideas don't need to be concrete, but it helps to start from a place of knowingness and objectivity.
2. Search for free plugins/themes within your WordPress dashboard and select four to six contenders. Install, activate, and evaluate them against your requirements. Narrow down your list to two selections and explore them further. If they don't meet your needs, repeat this step or consider searching for paid plugins/themes on the internet. If you take the latter step, purchase one theme at a time and experiment. If all else fails, review your requirements and make adjustments to find a plugin/theme that meets your needs.
3. Review your requirements on an ongoing basis and if things change, repeat steps one and two.

General Public License (GPLv2)

"The licenses for most software are designed to take away your freedom to share and change it. By contrast, the GNU General Public License is intended to guarantee your freedom to share and change free software—to make sure the software is free for all its users. This General Public License applies to most of the Free Software Foundation's software and to any other program whose authors commit to using it." –WordPress.org

Only recently did I engage in a debate about free versus paid plugins/themes in a Facebook group. It appears there are some hardcore WordPress users who believe paid solutions have no place in the open-source WordPress environment.

WordPress is an excellent platform, and users can find many exceptional free plugins/themes. However, WordPress also offers business opportunities for web designers and developers who want to make money—I think they call this capitalism. Even WordPress.org has added a commercial option on the themes tab for "GPL themes with extra paid services."

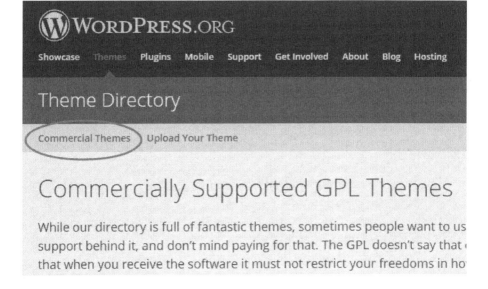

I'm glad I don't have to pay for every plugin I use, but I'm happy to invest in my online business through premium plugins and themes

that improve my website. GPL hippies must get over themselves and appreciate entrepreneurs seeking to deliver premium products that outperform free ones. People have bills to pay, and I appreciate developers who want to deliver game-changing products. If their solutions are worthwhile, they'll succeed. If their products suck, they'll fail.

How Many Plugins Are Too Many?

It's easy to go crazy with plugins, but how many is too many? According to Dan Norris of WP Curve, "As a general guide, we like to keep sites to under 20 plugins. A better rule of thumb is 'less is best.' If you can have zero, then that's fantastic but probably unrealistic. We have two recommendations here: remove any plugins you don't need and remove any inactive or active plugins that you don't need."

Dan and I might agree that having twenty to thirty plugins is enough to achieve desired goals. However, having fifty-three or 637 plugins are also possibilities. I have 18 plugins installed on digitalfodder.com, and every plugin serves a purpose.

Plugins can negatively affect website performance, page speed, security, and more. Review your plugins monthly or quarterly to ensure they remain necessary.

THE 672 BEST FREE PLUGINS

For this edition, plugins that met the following criteria where included.

- 60,000 or more active installs (previously 30,000)
- 10 or more reviews
- A four-star rating or better
- Updated within the past 12 months

A new is requirement is that a plugin must have been updated within the past 12 months. Frequently updated plugins tend to be more reliable, compatible, secure, and supported by their developers.

There are many excellent and unique plugins with less than 60,000 active installs, which I tried to include.

In a moment, you're going to sift through many amazing plugins. As any seasoned WordPress user knows, some plugin categories are more critical than others. For example, website administration, backup, SEO, and security categories should be top-of-mind for your site.

Although not highlighted in traditional hyperlink blue, plugins are clickable and will take you to the plugin's homepage on WordPress.org. I didn't correct the grammar for plugin titles and descriptions, so you'll find plenty of grammatical errors.

Ad Insert & Management Plugins (7)

Quick AdSense  Clickable Hyperlink

Quick AdSense offers a quicker & flexible way to insert Google AdSense or any Ads. >

WordPress Ads & AdSense plugin – Ad Inserter

Insert and manage ads: Google AdSense ads, Amazon banners, ad rotation, sticky widget ads, PHP. >

26

AdSense Plugin WP QUADS

Quick Adsense Reloaded! Quickest way to insert Google AdSense & other ads into your website. >

AdRotate Banner Manager

Monetise your website with adverts while keeping things simple. Start making money today! >

Advanced Ads

Manage and optimize your ads. All ad codes, Google AdSense Auto ads, ad widget, rotation. >

Wp-Insert

The Ultimate Adsense / Ad-Management Plugin for WordPress. >

Insert Post Ads

Automatically insert post ads after paragraphs of your posts, pages, and custom post types. >

Analytics & Statistics Plugins (10)

Google Analytics Dashboard for
WP by ExactMetrics (formerly
GADWP)

★★★★⯪ (379)

Connects Google Analytics with your
WordPress site. Displays stats to help
you understand your users...

ExactMetrics

1+ million active installations Tested with 5.0.2

Google Analytics Dashboard for WP

Connects Google Analytics with your WordPress site. Displays stats
to help you understand your users. >

WP Statistics

Complete WordPress Analytics and Statistics for your site! >

StatCounter – Free Real Time Visitor Stats

StatCounter.com powered real-time detailed stats about the visitors to
your blog. >

WP-PostViews

Enables you to display how many times a post/page had been viewed.
>

Slimstat Analytics

The leading web analytics plugin for WordPress. Track returning customers and registered users, monitor Javascript. >

Count per Day

Visit Counter, shows reads and visitors per page, visitors today, yesterday, last week, last months. >

Post Views Counter

Post Views Counter allows you to display how many times a post, page or custom. >

Statify

Visitor statistics for WordPress with focus on data protection, transparency and clarity. >

Google Analytics Counter Tracker

Google analytics counter tracker – analyse the visitors hits on you website and display it. >

Analytify – Google Analytics Dashboard Plugin for WordPress

Google Analytics for WordPress by Analytify is the must-have Plugin for Google Analytics! Now Enhanced. >

Backup Plugins (9)

UpdraftPlus WordPress Backup Plugin

★★★★★ (2,864)

Backup and restoration made easy. Complete backups; manual or scheduled (backup to Dropbox, S3, Google...

👤 UpdraftPlus.Com, DavidAnderson

📊 2+ million active installations ⓦ Tested with 5.0.2

UpdraftPlus WordPress Backup Plugin

Backup and restoration made easy. Complete backups; manual or scheduled (backup to Dropbox, S3, Google. >

Duplicator – WordPress Migration Plugin

WordPress migration and backups are much easier with Duplicator! Clone, backup, move and transfer an. >

BackWPup – WordPress Backup Plugin

Schedule complete automatic backups of your WordPress installation. Decide which content will be stored. >

WP-DB-Backup

On-demand backup of your WordPress database. >

BackUpWordPress

Simple automated backups of your WordPress-powered website. >

WordPress Backup and Migrate Plugin – Backup Guard

Backup site, restore or migrate it wherever you need it. >

XCloner – Backup and Restore

Backup your site, restore to any web location, send your backups to Dropbox, Amazon S3. >

WP Database Backup

Create & Restore Database Backup easily on single click. Manual or automated backups (backup to. >

Backup & Restore WPBackItUp

Backup, restore, clone, duplicate or migrate your site effortlessly with WPBackItUp. >

Cache Plugins (8)

WP Super Cache
★★★★⯪ (1,211)

A very fast caching engine for WordPress that produces static html files.

 Automattic

 2+ million active installations Tested with 5.0.2

WP Super Cache

A very fast caching engine for WordPress that produces static html files. >

W3 Total Cache

Search Engine (SEO) & Performance Optimization (WPO) via caching. Integrated caching: CDN, Minify, Page, Object. >

WP Fastest Cache

The simplest and fastest WP Cache system. >

LiteSpeed Cache

All-in-one unbeatable acceleration & PageSpeed improvement: caching, image/CSS/JS optimization. >

Nginx Helper

Cleans nginx's fastcgi/proxy cache or redis-cache whenever a post is edited/published. Also does a few. >

Cache Enabler – WordPress Cache

A lightweight caching plugin for WordPress that makes your website faster by generating static HTML. >

Hyper Cache

Hyper Cache is a performant and easy to configure cache system for WordPress. >

Redis Object Cache

A persistent object cache backend powered by Redis. Supports Predis, PhpRedis, HHVM, replication, clustering and. >

Calendar & Event Plugins (10)

The Events Calendar

★★★★☆ (1,611)

The Events Calendar is a carefully crafted, extensible plugin that lets you easily manage and...

Modern Tribe, Inc.

700,000+ active installations   Tested with 5.0.2

The Events Calendar

The Events Calendar is a carefully crafted, extensible plugin that lets you easily manage and. >

All-in-One Event Calendar

An events calendar system with multiple views, upcoming events widget, color-coded categories, recurrence, and import/export. >

Events Manager

Fully featured event registration management including recurring events, locations management, calendar, Google map integration. >

Comet Cache

Comet Cache is an advanced WordPress caching plugin inspired by simplicity. >

Editorial Calendar

The Editorial Calendar makes it possible to see all your posts and drag and drop. >

Event Organiser

Create and maintain events, including complex reoccurring patterns. >

Booking Calendar

Booking Calendar – original 1st booking plugin for WordPress. Easily receive reservations and show availability >

Calendar by WD – Responsive Event Calendar for WordPress

Event Calendar plugin is a highly configurable product which allows you to have multiple organized. >

My Calendar

Accessible WordPress event calendar plugin. Show events from multiple calendars on pages, in posts. >

Event Calendar WD – Responsive Event Calendar plugin

Event Calendar WD is a user-friendly event calendar plugin. This event calendar plugin allows organizing. >

CAPTCHA Plugins (3)

Really Simple CAPTCHA

★ ★ ★ ★ ½ (115)

Really Simple CAPTCHA is a CAPTCHA module intended to be called from other plugins. It...

 Takayuki Miyoshi

900,000+ active installations   Tested with 4.8.8

Really Simple CAPTCHA

Really Simple CAPTCHA does not work alone and is intended to work with other plugins. >

Google Captcha (reCAPTCHA) by BestWebSoft

Protect WordPress website forms from spam entries with Google reCaptcha. >

Invisible reCaptcha for WordPress

Invisible reCaptcha for WordPress plugin helps you to protect your sites against bad spam bots. >

Chat & Communication Plugins (7)

Tawk.to Live Chat

(OFFICIAL tawk.to plugin) Instantly chat with visitors on your website with the free tawk.to chat. >

Call Now Button

A very simple yet very effective plugin that adds a Call Now button to your site. >

Click to Chat for WhatsApp Chat

Let's make your Web page visitors Contact you through WhatsApp chat with a single click. >

WP Live Chat Support

Fully functional Live Chat plugin. Chat with your visitors for free! No need for monthly. >

WhatsHelp Chat Button

100% FREE website widget for chatting with your visitors via WhatsApp, Facebook Messenger. >

Tidio Live Chat

Meet Tidio Live Chat – a free live chat for your website. It integrates with. >

Live Chat with Facebook Messenger

Support your customers via Facebook Live Chat conveniently from your own website. Free Messenger Live. >

Contact Plugins (17)

Contact Form 7

★★★★⯨ (1,527)

Just another contact form plugin. Simple but flexible.

 Takayuki Miyoshi

 5+ million active installations ⓦ Tested with 5.0.2

Contact Form 7

Just another contact form plugin. Simple but flexible. >

Contact Widgets

Beautifully display social media and contact information on your website with these simple widgets. >

Contact Form by BestWebSoft

Simple contact form plugin any WordPress website must have. >

Contact Form & SMTP Plugin for WordPress by PirateForms

A simple and effective WordPress contact form & SMTP plugin. Compatible with best themes out. >

Flamingo

A trustworthy message storage plugin for Contact Form 7. >

Contact Form 7 Honeypot

Contact Form 7 Honeypot – Adds honeypot anti-spam functionality to CF7 forms. >

Visual Form Builder

Build beautiful, fully functional contact forms in only a few minutes without writing PHP, CSS, and more. >

Contact Form by WPForms – Drag & Drop Form Builder for WordPress

The best WordPress contact form plugin. Drag & Drop online form builder that helps you. >

Contact Form by WD – responsive drag & drop contact form builder tool

Contact Form by WD plugin is a simple contact form builder tool, which allows the. >

MW WP Form

MW WP Form is shortcode base contact form plugin. This plugin have many feature. >

Contact Bank – Contact Forms Builder

Contact Bank is an ultimate form builder WordPress plugin that lets you create contact forms. >

Bootstrap for Contact Form 7

This plugin modifies the output of the popular Contact Form 7 plugin to be styled. >

Contact Form 7 Database Addon – CFDB7

Save and manage Contact Form 7 messages. Never lose important data. It is lightweight contact. >

Contact Form 7 Redirection

A simple add-on for Contact Form 7 that adds a redirect option after form sent. >

Contact Form 7 Style

Simple style customization and templating for Contact Form 7 forms. Requires Contact Form 7 plugin. >

Conditional Fields for Contact Form 7

Adds conditional logic to Contact Form 7. >

Contact Form Clean and Simple

A clean and simple AJAX contact form with Google reCAPTCHA. >

Content Management Plugins (24)

Duplicate Post

Copy posts of any type with a click! >

Breadcrumb NavXT

Breadcrumb NavXT, the successor to the popular WordPress plugin Breadcrumb Navigation XT, was written from. >

Duplicate Page

Duplicate Posts, Pages and Custom Posts easily using single click. >

WP Edit

Take complete control over the WordPress content editor. >

Insert PHP

Run PHP code inserted into WordPress posts and pages. >

List Category Posts

List Category Posts allows you to list posts by category and many other parameters. >

Hide Title

Allows authors to hide the title on single pages and posts via the edit post. >

Advanced Excerpt

Control the appearance of WordPress post excerpts. >

Post Expirator

Allows you to add an expiration date to posts which you can configure to either. >

Post Type Switcher

A simple way to change a post's type in WordPress. >

Page-list

[pagelist], [subpages], [siblings] and [pagelist_ext] shortcodes. >

Content Views – Post Grid & List for WordPress

Create beautiful grid and list of WordPress posts, pages in minutes. No coding required. >

Page scroll to id

Create links that scroll the page smoothly to any id within the document. >

Pods – Custom Content Types and Fields

Pods is a framework for creating, managing, and deploying customized content types and fields. >

Show Hide Author

Choose whether to show or hide the author's name.

Advanced iFrame

Include content the way YOU like in an iframe that can hide and modify elements. >

Real-Time Find and Replace

Set up find and replace rules that are executed AFTER a page is generated by. >

Collapse-O-Matic

Remove clutter, save space: display and hide additional content in a SEO friendly way by. >

WP Meta and Date Remover

Remove meta author and date information from posts and pages. Hide from Humans and Search >

Public Post Preview

Enables you to give a link to anonymous users for public preview of a post. >

Tabby Responsive Tabs

Create responsive tabs inside your posts, pages or custom post content by adding simple shortcodes. >

Accordion

Create Accordion Content Beautifully on your WordPress. >

User Submitted Posts

Easily submit posts and images from the front-end of your site. >

Accordion FAQ

Accordion And Collapse is the most easiest drag & drop accordion builder for WordPress. >

Comment & Spam Plugins (10)

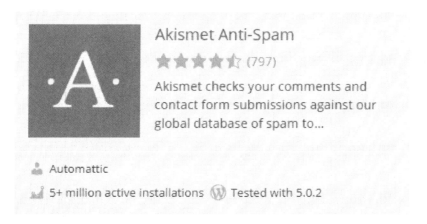

Akismet Anti-Spam

★★★★✫ (797)

Akismet checks your comments and contact form submissions against our global database of spam to...

Automattic

5+ million active installations   Tested with 5.0.2

Akismet

Akismet checks your comments and contact form submissions against our global database of spam to. >

Disable Comments

Allows administrators to globally disable comments on their site. Comments can be disabled according to. >

Antispam Bee

Antispam plugin with a sophisticated tool set for effective day to day comment and trackback. >

Anti-spam

No spam in comments. No captcha. >

Cerber Security, Antispam & Malware Scan

Protection against hacker attacks and bots. Malware scanner & integrity checker. User activity log. >

Spam protection, AntiSpam, FireWall by CleanTalk

Spam protection, anti-spam, all-in-one, premium plug-in. No spam comments & users, no spam contact. >

No Page Comment

An admin interface to control the default comment and trackback settings on new posts, pages. >

Stop Spammers

Aggressive anti-spam plugin that eliminates comment spam, trackback spam, contact form spam and registration spam. >

Comments – wpDiscuz

AJAX powered realtime comments. Designed to extend WordPress native comments. Custom comment forms and fields. >

Social Login

Allow your visitors to comment and login with social networks like Twitter, Facebook, Paypal, LinkedIn. >

Community & Membership Plugins (9)

bbPress

bbPress is forum software, made the WordPress way. >

BuddyPress

BuddyPress helps site builders and WordPress developers add community features to their websites. >

Members

The most powerful user, role, and capability management plugin for WordPress. >

WP-Members Membership Plugin

The WP-Members membership plugin turns your WordPress site into a membership site. >

Subscribe to Comments

Subscribe to Comments allows commenters on an entry to subscribe to e-mail notifications for subsequent.

Paid Memberships Pro

Get Paid with Paid Memberships Pro: The most complete member management and membership subscriptions plugin. >

Ultimate Member

The #1 user profile & membership plugin for WordPress. >

Simple Membership

Simple membership plugin adds membership functionality to your site. >

Groups

Groups is an efficient and powerful solution, providing group-based user membership management, group-based capabilities and. >

Cookie Notice, Consent & GDPR Plugins (11)

Cookie Notice for GDPR

Cookie Notice allows you to elegantly inform users that your site uses cookies and to. >

GDPR Cookie Consent

A simple way to get GDPR Cookie Consent as per EU GDPR/Cookie Law regulations. >

GDPR Cookie Consent Banner | Termly

Termly's easy to use cookie consent plugin can assist in your GDPR and ePrivacy Directive. >

EU Cookie Law

EU Cookie Law informs users that your site uses cookies, with option to lock scripts. >

Asesor de Cookies para normativa española

Este plugin le va a facilitar la confección de la política de cookies para. >

Shariff Wrapper

Shariff provides share buttons that respect the privacy of your visitors and follow the GDPR. >

GDPR Cookie Compliance

GDPR is an EU wide legislation that specifies how user data should be handled. >

Italy Cookie Choices (for EU Cookie Law)

Italy Cookie Choices allows you to easily comply with the european cookie law and block. >

Cookies for Comments

Sets a cookie on a random URL that is then checked when a comment is. >

GDPR

This plugin is meant to assist with the GDPR obligations of a Data processor. >

The GDPR Framework By Data443

Easy to use tools to help make your website GDPR-compliant. Fully documented, extendable and developer-friendly. >

CSS Plugins (10)

SiteOrigin CSS

SiteOrigin CSS is the simple, yet powerful CSS editor for WordPress. It gives you visual. >

Simple Custom CSS and JS

Easily add Custom CSS or JS to your website with an awesome editor. >

Forget About Shortcode Buttons

A visual way to add CSS buttons in the post editor screen and to your. >

Animate It!

Add cool CSS3 animations to your content. >

Simple Custom CSS

Add Custom CSS to your WordPress site without any hassles. >

WP Add Custom CSS

Add custom css to the whole website and to specific posts and pages. >

Simple CSS

Add CSS to your website through an admin editor, the Customizer or a metabox for. >

Insert Html Snippet

Add HTML, CSS and javascript code to your pages and posts easily using shortcodes. >

Visual CSS Style Editor

An advanced CSS editor which allows you edit the website design in real-time. >

Custom CSS and Javascript

Easily add custom CSS and Javascript code to your WordPress site, with draft previewing, revisions. >

Editors & Page Builders (42)

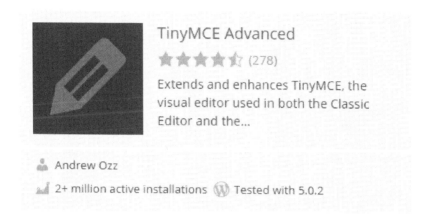

TinyMCE Advanced

★★★★⯪ (278)

Extends and enhances TinyMCE, the visual editor used in both the Classic Editor and the...

👤 Andrew Ozz

📊 2+ million active installations ⓦ Tested with 5.0.2

TinyMCE Advanced

Extends and enhances TinyMCE, the visual editor used in both the Classic Editor and the. >

Classic Editor

Enables the previous "classic" editor and the old-style Edit Post screen with TinyMCE, Meta Boxes. >

Disable Gutenberg

Disable Gutenberg Block Editor and restore the Classic Editor and original Edit Post screen. >

Black Studio TinyMCE Widget

The visual editor widget for WordPress. >

Redux Framework

Redux is a simple, truly extensible and fully responsive options framework for WordPress themes and. >

Genesis Simple Edits

This plugin lets you edit the three most commonly modified areas in any Genesis theme. >

Page Builder by SiteOrigin

Build responsive page layouts using the widgets you know and love using this simple drag. >

Beaver Builder – WordPress Page Builder

The best drag and drop WordPress Page Builder. Easily build beautiful home pages, professional landing. >

Child Theme Configurator

When using the Customizer is not enough – Create a child theme from your installed. >

AddQuicktag

This plugin makes it easy to add Quicktags to the html – and visual-editor. >

Spacer

Adds a spacer button to the WYSIWYG visual editor. >

Kirki

The ultimate toolkit for theme developers using the WordPress Customizer. >

Responsive Menu

Highly customisable Responsive Menu plugin with 150+ options. >

Unyson

A simple and easy way to build a powerful website. >

WP Responsive Menu

WP Responsive Menu turns your WordPress menu to a highly customizable sliding responsive menu. >

SiteOrigin Widgets by CodeLights

Flexible high-end shortcodes and widgets. Responsive, modern, SEO-optimized and easy-to-use. >

Page Builder: Live Composer – drag and drop website builder (visual front-end site editor)

Front-end page builder for WordPress with drag and drop editing. Build PRO responsive websites and. >

Sticky Menu (or Anything!) on Scroll

Sticky Menu (Or Anything!) On Scroll will let you choose any element on your page. >

WPFront Scroll Top

WPFront Scroll Top plugin allows the visitor to easily scroll back to the top of. >

To Top

To Top is a nifty lightweight plugin. It adds a highly customizable button, which when. >

jQuery Smooth Scroll

Activate the plugin for smooth scrolling and smooth "back to top" feature. >

Nested Pages

Nested Pages provides a drag and drop interface for managing pages & posts in the. >

MCE Table Buttons

Adds table editing controls to the visual content editor (TinyMCE). >

Re-add text underline and justify

Version 0.2 adds support for Gutenberg for its "Classic" bloc only. >

Page Builder: KingComposer – Free Drag and Drop page builder by King-Theme

Lightweight and extremely powerful Page Builder. Allow you to easily create pages like a true. >

HTML Editor Syntax Highlighter

Add syntax highlighting to the classic WordPress code editors using Codemirror.js. >

Brizy – Page Builder

Creating WordPress pages should be fast & easy. Brizy is a new and innovative way. >

Team Members

A responsive and clean way to display your team. Create members, add their positions, bios. >

Timber

Helps you create themes faster with sustainable code. With Timber, you write HTML using Twig. >

Blog Designer

Allows you to create and modify your blog page with 6 unique blog layouts. >

Elementor Page Builder

The most advanced frontend drag & drop page builder. Create high-end, pixel perfect websites. >

Essential Addons for Elementor

Ultimate elements library for Elementor WordPress Page Builder. 54+ Premium elements with endless customization options. >

Header, Footer & Blocks for Elementor

Create Header and Footer for your site using Elementor Page Builder. >

Premium Addons for Elementor

Elementor Widgets and Addons like Grid, Modal Box, Carousel, Google Maps, Pricing Tables, Countdown, Testimonials. >

Elementor Addons & Templates – Sizzify Lite

Adds new Addons & Widgets that are specifically designed to be used in conjunction with. >

Elementor Addon Elements

Add new elements to Elementor page builder. >

NavMenu Addon For Elementor

Adds new NavMenus to the Elementor Page Builder plugin. Now with Site Branding options. >

Livemesh Addons for Elementor

A collection of premium quality addons or modules for use in Elementor page builder. >

Page Templater For Elementor

A helper plugin for users of Elementor Page Builder. >

Contact Form7 Widget For Elementor Page Builder

This WordPress Plugin Adds Contact Form 7 widget element to Elementor page builder for easy. >

AnyWhere Elementor

Insert Elementor created content anywhere using shortcode. Insert Elementor created content anywhere using shortcode. >

Tabs

Tabs Responsive is the most easiest drag & drop Tabs builder for WordPress. You can. >

E-Mail & SMTP Plugins (13)

WP Mail SMTP by WPForms

★★★★½ (331)

The most popular WordPress SMTP and PHP Mailer plugin. Trusted by over 1 million sites.

WPForms

1+ million active installations Tested with 5.0.2

WP Mail SMTP

The most popular WordPress SMTP and PHP Mailer plugin. Trusted by over 1 million sites. >

MailPoet – emails and newsletters in WordPress

Send beautiful newsletters from WordPress. Collect subscribers with signup forms, automate your emails for WooCommerce. >

Newsletter

Add a real newsletter system to your blog. For free. With unlimited newsletters and subscribers. >

Easy WP SMTP

Easily send emails from your WordPress blog using your preferred SMTP server. >

Post SMTP Mailer/Email Log

Send, log and troubleshoot your Outgoing Email easily. Supports everything: SMTP, Gmail, Mailgun, Mandril, SendGrid. >

Genesis eNews Extended

Creates a new widget to easily add mailing lists integration to a Genesis website. >

Email Address Encoder

A lightweight plugin to protect email addresses from email-harvesting robots by encoding them into decimal. >

WP SMTP

WP SMTP can help us to send emails via SMTP instead of the PHP mail(). >

Contact Form 7 MailChimp Extension

Simple way to integrate MailChimp mailing lists to Contact Form 7. >

WP Mail SMTP Plugin with Email Logs

Mail Bank is a wordpress smtp plugin that solves email deliverability issue. Configures Gmail Smtp. >

WP Mail Logging

Logs each email sent by WordPress. >

SMTP Mailer

Configure a SMTP server to send email from your WordPress site. Configure the wp_mail() function. >

Email Encoder Bundle – Protect Email Address

Encode mailto links, email addresses, phone numbers and any text to hide them from (spam)bots. >

Form & Opt-in Form Plugins (20)

Ninja Forms – The Easy and Powerful Forms Builder

★★★★½ (940)

Drag and drop fields in an intuitive UI to create contact forms, email subscription forms....

👤 The WP Ninjas

📊 1+ million active installations 🐵 Tested with 5.0.2

Ninja Forms

Drag and drop fields in an intuitive UI to create contact forms, email subscription forms. >

MailChimp for WordPress

MailChimp for WordPress, the #1 MailChimp plugin. >

Proven Strategies To Automate Your Ecommerce Growth

Sumo is trusted by over 600,000 businesses — small and large — in growing their. >

Email Subscribers & Newsletters

Add subscription forms on website, send HTML newsletters & automatically notify subscribers about new blog. >

MailChimp Forms by MailMunch

MailChimp Forms to get more email subscribers. >

Easy Forms for MailChimp

The ultimate MailChimp WordPress plugin. Easily build unlimited forms for your MailChimp lists, add them. >

Contact Forms, Surveys & Quiz Forms Plugin by Formidable

The most advanced WordPress forms plugin. Go beyond contact forms with our drag & drop. >

Form Maker by WD

Form Maker is a user-friendly contact form builder that allows to create forms for any. >

Form Builder

Form Builder is an intuitive tool for creating contact forms rearranging and editing fields. >

Hustle – Pop-Ups, Slide-ins and Email Opt-ins

The complete marketing plugin for email opt-ins, pop-up advertising and building your user base. >

Caldera Forms – More Than Contact Forms

Responsive form builder for contact forms, user registration and login forms, Mailchimp. >

Web-Settler Forms – Create Responsive Contact Forms

Contact form saves your hours of precious time by making contact form creation process super. >

Popups – WordPress Popup

Popup plugin that works! Most complete free popup plugin with display filters, scroll triggered popups. >

Popups, Welcome Bar, Optins and Lead Generation Plugin – Icegram

The best WP popup plugin that let's you create a popup within seconds. Customize popup. >

Popup Maker

Everything you need to create unique user experiences. Insert forms & other content from your. >

Contact Form Builder for WordPress – Conversion Tools by HubSpot

The Contact Form Builder plugin, a part of HubSpot's Conversion Tools, allows you to create. >

Popup by Supsystic

Popup by Supsystic is the best way to convert visitors into subscribers, followers & customers. >

MailMunch – Grow your Email List

The best free plugin to get more email subscribers. Beautiful opt-in forms that integrate with. >

Boxzilla

Flexible call to action boxes, popping up or sliding in at just the right time. >

Form Builder | Create Responsive Contact Forms

Form builder is a user friendly drag & drop plugin. This Form Builder will let. >

Favicon (2)

All In One Favicon

Easily add a Favicon to your site and the WordPress admin pages. >

Favicon by RealFaviconGenerator

Create and install your favicon for all platforms: PC/Mac, iPhone/iPad, Android devices, Windows 8 tablets. >

Font Plugins (6)

Easy Google Fonts

Adds google fonts to any theme without coding and integrates with the WordPress Customizer automatically. >

Better Font Awesome

The Better Font Awesome plugin for WordPress. Shortcodes, HTML, TinyMCE, various Font Awesome versions, backwards. >

Use Any Font [Freemium]

Embed any custom font in your website. #1 Rated custom fonts plugin by WPMUDev.org. >

Disable Google Fonts

Disable enqueuing of fonts from Google used by WordPress core, default themes, Gutenberg, and many. >

WP SVG Icons

Quickly and effortlessly enable 490+ beautifully designed SVG font icons, available on the frontend and. >

Google Fonts for WordPress

The easiest to use Google Fonts plugin. No coding required. 870+ font choices. Now includes. >

Image & Media Plugins (44)

 Regenerate Thumbnails

★ ★ ★ ★ ☆ (323)

Regenerate the thumbnails for one or more of your image uploads. Useful when changing their...

 Alex Mills (Viper007Bond)

 1+ million active installations Tested with 5.0.2

Regenerate Thumbnails

Regenerate the thumbnails for one or more of your image uploads. Useful when changing their. >

WordPress Gallery Plugin – NextGEN Gallery

The most popular WordPress gallery plugin and one of the most popular plugins of all. >

Image Widget

A simple image widget that uses the native WordPress media manager to add image widgets. >

EWWW Image Optimizer

Speed up your website and improve your visitors' experience by automatically compressing and resizing images. >

Photo Gallery by 10Web – Responsive Photo Gallery for WordPress

Photo Gallery is a powerful image gallery plugin with a list of advanced options for. >

Easy FancyBox

Easily enable the FancyBox jQuery extension on just about all media links. Multi-Site compatible. >

Responsive Lightbox & Gallery

Responsive Lightbox & Gallery allows users to create galleries and view larger versions of images. >

Enable Media Replace

Easily replace any attached image/file by simply uploading a new file in the Media Library. >

Imsanity

Imsanity automatically resizes huge image uploads. Are contributors uploading huge photos? Tired of manually scaling? >

Simple Lightbox

The highly customizable lightbox for WordPress. >

iframe

Speedup and protect WordPress in a smart way. >

AJAX Thumbnail Rebuild

AJAX Thumbnail Rebuild allows you to rebuild all thumbnails at once without script timeouts on your site. >

FancyBox for WordPress

Seamlessly integrates FancyBox into your blog: Upload, activate, and you're done. >

Enhanced Media Library

The plugin will be handy for those who need to manage a lot of media. >

Add From Server

"Add From Server" is a quick plugin which allows you to import media & files. >

Simple Image Sizes

This plugin allow create custom image sizes for your site. Override your theme sizes directly. >

WordPress Photo Gallery Plugin – Envira Gallery

Envira Gallery is the fastest, easiest to use WordPress image gallery plugin. Lightbox with Drag. >

FooGallery – Image Gallery WordPress Plugin

Why choose FooGallery? Stunning gallery layouts, responsive, retina-ready, lightning fast, easy to use. Gutenberg Ready! >

WordPress Button Plugin MaxButtons

WordPress button plugin so powerful and easy to use anyone can create beautiful buttons. >

SVG Support

Upload SVG files to the Media Library and render SVG files inline for direct styling/animation. >

Dynamic Featured Image

Dynamically adds multiple featured image (post thumbnail) functionality to posts, pages and custom post types. >

jQuery Colorbox

Adds Colorbox/Lightbox functionality to images, grouped by post or page. Works for. >

Get the Image

An easy-to-use image script for adding things such as thumbnail, slider, gallery, and feature images. >

Multiple Post Thumbnails

Adds multiple post thumbnails to a post type. If you've ever wanted more than one. >

Photo Gallery by Supsystic

Photo Gallery with visual editor to build amazing photo gallery. >

Gallery – Portfolio Gallery

Gallery – Portfolio Gallery is a great plugin for adding specialized portfolio galleriey, video portfolio.

Post Thumbnail Editor

Fed up with the lack of automated tools to properly crop and scale post thumbnails? >

Resize Image After Upload

Automatically resize your images after upload using this plugin. >

WP Photo Album Plus

This plugin is more than just a photo album plugin, it is a complete, highly. >

Media Library Assistant

Enhances the Media Library. >

Image Gallery by Robo – Responsive Photo Gallery

Robo Gallery is advanced responsive photo gallery plugin. Flexible gallery images management tools. Links, videos. >

Slideshow Gallery

Feature content in a JavaScript powered slideshow gallery showcase on your WordPress website. >

Responsive Photo Gallery for WordPress by Gallery Bank

Gallery Bank is an advanced plugin which creates Beautiful Photo Galleries and Albums for different. >

Gallery – Flagallery Photo Portfolio

Gallery Portfolio, Photo Gallery, Video Gallery, Music Album & Banner Rotator plugin with powerfull admin. >

Image Watermark

Image Watermark allows you to automatically watermark images uploaded to the WordPress Media Library and. >

Easy Watermark

Allows to add watermark to images automatically on upload or manually. >

Attachments

Attachments allows you to simply append any number of items from your WordPress Media Library. >

WP Featherlight – A Simple jQuery Lightbox

An ultra-lightweight jQuery lightbox for WordPress images and galleries. >

Pixabay Images

Find quality CC0 Public Domain images for commercial use, and add them to your blog. >

Modula Image Gallery

Photo Gallery by Modula – an advanced solution for Photo Gallery users. Create beautiful image. >

Media File Renamer Auto

Physically renames your files nicely for a cleaner system and for a better SEO. >

Image Photo Gallery Final Tiles Grid

Image Gallery + Photo Gallery + Portfolio Gallery + Tiled Gallery in 1 plugin. Includes. >

Tiled Gallery Carousel Without JetPack

Tiled Gallery Carousel allows you to display image galleries in mosaic styles without Jetpack. >

Slideshow Gallery

Feature content in a JavaScript powered slideshow gallery showcase on your WordPress website. >

Language & Translation Plugins (8)

Loco Translate

Translate WordPress plugins and themes directly in your browser. >

Polylang

Making WordPress multilingual. >

Google Language Translator

Welcome to Google Language Translator! This plugin allows you to insert the Google Language Translator. >

Translate WordPress with GTranslate

Translate WordPress with Google Translate multilanguage plugin to make your website multilingual. >

TranslatePress – Translate Multilingual sites

Easily translate your entire site directly from the front-end and go multilingual, with full support. >

Translate WP website – Weglot Translate

Translate your website into multiple languages without any code. Weglot Translate is fully SEO compatible. >

WPGlobus – Multilingual Everything!

Multilingual/Globalization: URL-based multilanguage; easy translation interface, compatible with Gutenberg, Yoast SEO, All in One SEO. >

Transposh WordPress Translation

Transposh adds best of breed translation support to wordpress, 117 languages are automatically translated and. >

Login Plugins (6)

Nextend Social Login and Register (Facebook, Google, Twitter)

One click registration & login plugin for Facebook, Google, Twitter and more. Quick setup. >

Login With Ajax

Add smooth ajax login/registration effects and choose where users get redirected upon log in/out. >

Theme My Login

Themes the WordPress login pages according to your theme. >

Login Logo

Customize the logo on the WP login screen by simply dropping a file named login-logo.png. >

Erident Custom Login and Dashboard

Customize completely your WordPress Login Screen easily. Add your logo, change background image, colors, styles. >

Customize WordPress Login Page

Customize Your WordPress Login Screen Amazingly – Add Own Logo, Add Social Profiles, Login Form. >

Map Plugins (13)

WP Google Maps

The easiest to use Google maps plugin! Create a custom Google map with high quality. >

MapPress Maps for WordPress

MapPress adds beautiful, interactive Google or Leaflet maps to WordPress. >

Google Maps Widget

Google Maps taking forever to load? Try Google Maps Widget. >

Comprehensive Google Map Plugin

A simple and intuitive, yet elegant and fully documented Google map plugin that installs as. >

WP Google Map Plugin

A Responsive Google Maps plugin to display custom markers on the google maps and show. >

Snazzy Maps

Apply styles to your Google Maps with the official Snazzy Maps WordPress plugin. >

API KEY for Google Maps

Retroactively add Google Maps API KEY to any theme or plugin. >

WordPress Google Maps Plugin

A simple, easy and quite powerful Google Maps tool to create, manage and embed custom. >

Simple Map

Easy way to embed google map(s). >

Google Maps Easy

Google Maps with markers, locations and clusterization. >

WP Store Locator

An easy to use location management system that enables users to search for nearby physical. >

Leaflet Maps Marker (Google Maps, OpenStreetMap, Bing Maps)

The most comprehensive & user-friendly mapping solution for WordPress. >

Maps Builder – Google Maps Plugin

The most flexible, robust, and easy to use WordPress plugin for creating powerful Google Maps. >

Miscellaneous & Multipurpose (34)

WP Multibyte Patch

Multibyte functionality enhancement for the WordPress Japanese package. >

Orbit Fox by ThemeIsle

This swiss-knife plugin comes with a quality template library, menu/sharing icons, Gutenberg blocks and newly. >

DuracellTomi's Google Tag Manager for WordPress

The first Google Tag Manager plugin for WordPress with business goals in mind. >

WP Job Manager

Manage job listings from the WordPress admin panel, and allow users to post job listings. >

Download Monitor

Download Monitor is a plugin for uploading and managing downloads, tracking downloads, and displaying links. >

PDF Embedder

Embed PDFs straight into your posts and pages, with intelligent resizing of width and height. >

Auto Terms of Service and Privacy Policy

Create Privacy Policy (Simple or GDPR), Terms & Conditions, Disclaimers and more. >

Import any XML or CSV File to WordPress

WP All Import is an extremely powerful importer that makes it easy to import any. >

OneSignal – Web Push Notifications

Increase engagement and drive more repeat traffic to your WordPress site with desktop push notifications.>

Disable Emojis (GDPR friendly)

This plugin disables the new WordPress emoji functionality. GDPR friendly. >

One Click Demo Import

Import your demo content, widgets and theme settings with one click. Theme authors! Enable simple. >

Heartbeat Control

Allows you to easily manage the frequency of the WordPress heartbeat API. >

PowerPress Podcasting plugin by Blubrry

No. 1 Podcasting plugin for WordPress, with simple & advanced modes, players, subscribe tools, and. >

Easy Digital Downloads

The easiest way to sell digital products with WordPress. >

WP Retina 2x

Make your website look beautiful and crisp on modern displays by creating and displaying retina images. >

Easy Smooth Scroll Links

Easy Smooth Scroll Links adds scroll animation effects to page anchors, smooth scroll and more. >

No Self Pings

Keeps WordPress from sending pings to your own site. >

Compact WP Audio Player

A Compact WP Audio Player Pluign that is compatible with all major browsers and devices. >

WP RSS Aggregator

WP RSS Aggregator is the original & most popular WordPress solution for importing RSS feeds. >

Ditty News Ticker

Ditty News Ticker is a multi-functional data display plugin. >

Gwolle Guestbook

Gwolle Guestbook is the WordPress guestbook you've just been looking for. Beautiful and easy. >

Embed Any Document

Easiest way to upload and display PDF, MS Office and more documents on your WordPress. >

WordPress Ping Optimizer

Save your WordPress blog from getting tagged as ping spammer. >

Give – Donation Plugin and Fundraising Platform

Accept donations and begin fundraising with Give, the highest rated WordPress donation plugin for online. >

PayPal Donations

Easy, simple setup to add a PayPal Donation button as a Widget or with a. >

Disable Feeds

Disables all RSS/Atom/RDF feeds on your WordPress site. >

Ultimate FAQ

FAQ plugin that lets you easily create, order and publicize FAQs using shortcodes, with many. >

WordPress Charts and Graphs Lite

A simple and quite powerful WordPress chart plugin to create and embed interactive charts. >

Reduce HTTP Requests, Disable Emojis & Disable Embeds, Speedup WooCommerce

Reduce HTTP requests – Disable Emojis, Disable Gravatars, Disable Embeds. >

FEEDZY RSS Feeds Lite

FEEDZY RSS Feeds is an easy-to-use plugin giving you RSS aggregator and autoblogging functionality. >

WP-Print

Displays a printable version of your WordPress blog's post/page. >

Quotes Collection

Quotes Collection plugin with Ajax powered Random Quote sidebar widget helps you collect and display. >

Business Directory Plugin

Build any kind of local directory, directory of business providers, a Yellow-Pages business directory, Yelp-like. >

Google Doc Embedder

Let's you embed PDF, MS Office, and many other file types in a web page. >

Notification Bars (3)

WPFront Notification Bar

Easily lets you create a bar on top or bottom to display a notification. >

WP Notification Bars

Create custom notification and alert bar for marketing promotions, alerts, increasing click throughs to other. >

Simple Banner

This plugin makes it easy to display a simple announcement banner or bar at the top of your website. >

Online Course Management (1)

LearnPress – WordPress LMS Plugin

A WordPress LMS Plugin to create WordPress Learning Management System. Turn your WP to LMS. >

Poll, Rating, Survey, and Testimonial Plugins (14)

WP-Polls

Adds an AJAX poll system to your WordPress blog. >

WP-PostRatings

Adds an AJAX rating system for your WordPress site's content. >

WP Product Review Lite

Easily turn your basic posts into in-depth reviews with ratings, pros and cons, affiliate links. >

WP Customer Reviews

Allows your visitors to leave business / product reviews. >

Testimonials Widget

Easily add social proofing to your website with Testimonials Widget. List or slide reviews via. >

kk Star Ratings

kk Star Ratings allows blog visitors to involve and interact more effectively with your website. >

Easy Testimonials

Testimonials widget and shortcode for adding Testimonials to your WordPress Theme, with a simple interface. >

Testimonial Rotator

Easily add Testimonials to your WordPress Blog or Company Website. >

Strong Testimonials

Simple yet powerful. Very customizable. Developer-friendly. Strong support. >

Quiz And Survey Master (Formerly Quiz Master Next)

Easily and quickly add unlimited quizzes and surveys to your website. >

Yasr – Yet Another Stars Rating

Boost the way people interact with your website, e-commerce or blog with an easy and. >

YOP Poll

Use a full option polling solution to get the answers you need. >

WP ULike

WP ULike enables you to add Ajax Like button into your WP and allowing your. >

Google Reviews Widget

Google Reviews Widget show Google Places Reviews on your WordPress website to increase user confidence. >

Popular, Recent, & Related Post Plugins (11)

WordPress Popular Posts

A highly customizable, easy-to-use popular posts widget! >

Yet Another Related Posts Plugin (YARPP)

Display a list of related posts on your site based on a powerful unique algorithm.

Recent Posts Widget Extended

Provides flexible and advanced recent posts. Display it via shortcode or widget with thumbnails, post. >

Recent Posts Widget With Thumbnails

List the most recent posts with post titles, thumbnails, excerpts, authors, categories, dates and more! >

Contextual Related Posts

Add related posts to your WordPress site with inbuilt caching. >

Related Posts

Related posts a so easy and fast. >

Related Posts for WordPress

Display related posts without slowing down your website! Link all your existing content with only. >

Top 10 – Popular posts plugin for WordPress

Track daily and total visits on your blog posts. Display the count as well as. >

Related Posts

Related Posts is The Best Customizable plugin, that nicely displays related posts thumbnails under the. >

Related Posts Thumbnails Plugin for WordPress

Related Posts by WPBrigade is The Best Customizable plugin, that nicely displays related posts thumbnails. >

Inline Related Posts

Inline Related Posts AUTOMATICALLY inserts related posts INSIDE your content, capturing immediately the reader's attention. >

Redirection & Link Management Plugins (16)

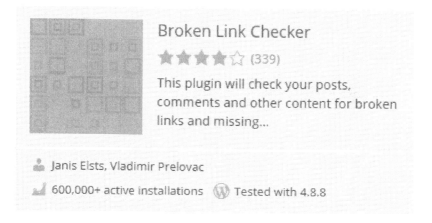

Broken Link Checker
★★★★☆ (339)
This plugin will check your posts, comments and other content for broken links and missing...

Janis Elsts, Vladimir Prelovac
600,000+ active installations   Tested with 4.8.8

Broken Link Checker

This plugin will check your posts, comments and other content for broken links and missing. >

Redirection

Manage 301 redirections, keep track of 404 errors, and improve your site, with no knowledge. >

Page Links To

Lets you make a WordPress page (or port or other content type) link to a. >

Simple 301 Redirects

Simple 301 Redirects provides an easy method of redirecting requests to another page on your site. >

Shortlinks by Pretty Links – Best WordPress Link Tracking Plugin

Shrink, beautify, track, manage and share any URL on or off of your WordPress website. >

Velvet Blues Update URLs

Updates all URLs and content links in your website. >

Custom Permalinks

Set custom permalinks on a per-post, per-tag or per-category basis. >

Custom Post Type Permalinks

Edit the permalink of custom post type. >

No Category Base (WPML)

This plugin removes the mandatory 'Category Base' from your category permalinks. >

Easy HTTPS Redirection

The plugin allows an automatic redirection to the "HTTPS" version/URL of the site. >

Remove Category URL

This plugin removes '/category' from your category permalinks. (e.g. /category/my-category/ to /my-category/) >

Safe Redirect Manager

Safely and easily manage your website's HTTP redirects. >

Open external links in a new window

Opens all (or specific) external links in a new window. XHTML Strict compliant and search. >

404page – your smart custom 404 error page

Custom 404 the easy way! Set any page as custom 404 error page. No coding. >

Go Live Update URLS

Goes through entire site and replaces all instances of and old url with a new. >

ThirstyAffiliates Affiliate Link Manager

Affiliate link management & cloaker tool. Easily manage, shrink and track your affiliate links in. >

Security Plugins (26)

Wordfence Security – Firewall & Malware Scan

★★★★★ (3,326)

Secure your website with the most comprehensive WordPress security plugin. Firewall, malware scan, blocking, live...

 Wordfence

 2+ million active installations Tested with 5.0.2

Wordfence Security

Secure your website with the most comprehensive WordPress security plugin. Firewall, malware scan, blocking, live. >

iThemes Security (formerly Better WP Security)

iThemes Security is the #1 WordPress Security Plugin >

All in One WP Security & Firewall

A comprehensive, user-friendly, all in one WordPress security and firewall plugin for your site. >

Loginizer

Loginizer is a WordPress security plugin which helps you fight against bruteforce attacks. >

Sucuri Security – Auditing, Malware Scanner and Security Hardening

The Sucuri WordPress Security plugin is a security toolset for security integrity monitoring, malware detection. >

MainWP Child

Provides a secure connection between your MainWP Dashboard and your WordPress sites. >

Login LockDown

Limits the number of login attempts from a given IP range within a certain time. >

Anti-Malware Security and Brute-Force Firewall

This Anti-Malware scanner searches for Malware, Viruses, and other security threats and vulnerabilities on your website. >

Really Simple SSL

No setup required! You only need an SSL certificate, and this plugin will do the. >

Password Protected

A very simple way to quickly password protect your WordPress site with a single password. >

WPS Hide Login

Change wp-login.php to anything you want. >

BulletProof Security

WordPress Security Protection: Malware scanner, Firewall, Login Security, DB Backup, Anti-Spam & much more. >

WordPress HTTPS (SSL)

WordPress HTTPS is intended to be an all-in-one solution to using SSL on WordPress sites. >

Theme Authenticity Checker

Scan all of your theme files for potentially malicious or unwanted code. >

SSL Insecure Content Fixer

Clean up WordPress website HTTPS insecure content. >

Peter's Login Redirect

Redirect users to different locations after logging in and logging out. >

BBQ: Block Bad Queries

The fastest firewall plugin for WordPress. >

Custom Login Page Customizer

Custom Login Customizer allows you to easily customize your admin login page, straight from your. >

WP Content Copy Protection & No Right Click

This wp plugin protect the posts content from being copied by any other web site. >

Shield Security for WordPress

Complete All-In-One Protection for your WordPress sites, that makes Security Easy for Everyone. >

WP Security Audit Log

An easy to use & comprehensive WordPress activity log plugin to log all changes on. >

CloudFlare Flexible SSL

Fix For CloudFlare Flexible SSL Redirect Loop For WordPress. >

WP Force SSL

This plugin helps you redirect HTTP traffic to HTTPS without the need of touching any. >

Safe SVG

Enable SVG uploads and sanitize them to stop XML/SVG vulnerabilities in your WordPress website. >

Hide My Site

Choose a single password to protect your entire wordpress site from the public and search. >

IP Geo Block

It blocks spam posts, login attempts and malicious access to the back-end requested from the. >

SEO & Search Plugins (15)

Yoast SEO

★★★★★ (24,356)

Improve your WordPress SEO: Write better content and have a fully optimized WordPress site using...

 Team Yoast

 5+ million active installations Tested with 5.0.2

Yoast SEO

Improve your WordPress SEO: Write better content and have a fully optimized WordPress site using. >

All in One SEO Pack

The original WordPress SEO plugin, downloaded over 50,000,000 times since 2007. >

ACF Content Analysis for Yoast SEO

WordPress plugin that adds the content of all ACF fields to the Yoast SEO score. >

Search & Replace

Search & Replace data in your database with WordPress admin, replace domains/URLs of your WordPress. >

Relevanssi – A Better Search

Relevanssi replaces the default search with a partial-match search that sorts results by relevance. >

All In One Schema.org Rich Snippets

Get eye catching results in search engines with the most popular schema markup plugin. >

Glue for Yoast SEO & AMP

This plugin makes sure the default WordPress AMP plugin uses the proper Yoast SEO metadata. >

Better Search Replace

A simple plugin to update URLs or other text in a database. >

The SEO Framework

The SEO Framework plugin provides an automated and advanced SEO solution for your WordPress website. >

WP SEO Structured Data Schema

Comprehensive JSON-LD based Structured Data solution for WordPress for adding schema for organizations, businesses, blog. >

SmartCrawl SEO

The SEO checker and optimization tool that helps you rank higher and get discovered in. >

Ajax Search Lite

A powerful ajax search engine for WordPress. Add a live search form to your site. >

Search & Filter

Search and Filtering for Custom Posts, Categories, Tags, Taxonomies, Post Dates and Post Types. >

SEOPress

SEOPress is a simple, fast and powerful SEO plugin for WordPress.
>

Search Exclude

Hide any post or page from the search results. >

Shortcode & Code Plugins (19)

Shortcodes Ultimate
★★★★★ (4,744)
A comprehensive collection of visual components for your site

Vladimir Anokhin
800,000+ active installations   Tested with 5.0.2

Shortcodes Ultimate

A comprehensive collection of visual components for your site. >

Display Posts Shortcode

Display a listing of posts using the [display-posts] shortcode. >

PHP code snippets (Insert PHP)

This plugin helps to use php code snippets in admin area without adding this code. >

Bootstrap Shortcodes for WordPress

Implements Bootstrap 3 styles and components in WordPress through shortcodes. >

Posts in Page

Easily add one or more posts to any page using simple shortcodes. >

Code Snippets

An easy, clean and simple way to add code snippets to your site. >

Column Shortcodes

Adds shortcodes to easily create columns in your posts or pages. >

Shortcoder

Create custom "Shortcodes" easily for HTML, JavaScript snippets and use the shortcodes within posts, pages. >

Post Snippets

Create custom shortcodes and reusable content and insert them in into your posts and pages. >

Site Administration Plugins (78)

Advanced Custom Fields

★ ★ ★ ★ ★ (1,041)

Customize WordPress with powerful, professional and intuitive fields.

Elliot Condon

1+ million active installations | Tested with 4.9.9

Advanced Custom Fields

Customize WordPress with powerful, professional and intuitive fields. >

WP-PageNavi

Adds a more advanced paging navigation interface. >

Post Types Order

Post Order and custom Post Type Objects (custom post types) using a Drag and Drop. >

Custom Post Type UI

Admin UI for creating custom post types and custom taxonomies for WordPress. >

InfiniteWP Client

Install this plugin on unlimited sites and manage them all from a central dashboard. >

ManageWP Worker

A better way to manage dozens of WordPress websites. >

All-in-One WP Migration

Move, transfer, copy, migrate, and backup a site with 1-click. Quick, easy, and reliable. >

Simple Page Ordering

Order your pages and other hierarchical post types with simple drag and drop. >

Toolset Types

The complete and reliable plugin for managing custom post types, custom taxonomies and custom fields. >

Category Order and Taxonomy Terms Order

Order Categories and all custom taxonomies terms (hierarchically) and child terms using a drag and drop. >

Meta Box

Meta Box plugin is a powerful, professional developer toolkit to create custom meta boxes. >

WP Migrate DB

Migrates your database by running find & replace on URLs and file paths, handling serialized. >

Admin Menu Editor

Let's you edit the WordPress admin menu. You can re-order, hide or rename menus, add. >

Insert Headers and Footers

This plugin allows you to add extra scripts to the header and footer of your site. >

Intuitive Custom Post Order

Intuitively, order items (Posts, Pages, and Custom Post Types, and Custom Taxonomies) using a drag. >

WP-DBManager

Manages your WordPress database. >

Easy Theme and Plugin Upgrades

Easily upgrade your themes and plugins using zip files without removing the theme or plugin. >

Max Mega Menu

An easy to use mega menu plugin. Written the WordPress way. >

Simple Custom Post Order

Order posts (posts, any custom post types) using a Drag and Drop Sortable JavaScript. >

Theme Check

A simple and easy way to test your theme for all the latest WordPress standards. >

White Label CMS

Customize dashboard panels and branding, hide menus plus lots more. >

Options Framework

The Options Framework Plugin makes it easy to include an options panel in any WordPress. >

Head, Footer and Post Injections

Header and Footer plugin let you to add html code to the head and footer. >

Easy Updates Manager

Manage all your WordPress updates, including individual updates, automatic updates, logs, and loads more. >

CMB2

CMB2 is a metabox, custom fields, and forms library for WordPress that will blow your mind. >

Post Duplicator

Creates functionality to duplicate any and all post types, including taxonomies & custom fields. >

Revision Control

Revision Control allows finer control over the Post Revision system included with WordPress. >

Menu Icons by ThemeIsle

Spice up your navigation menus with pretty icons, easily. >

Header and Footer Scripts

Header and Footer Scripts plugin allows you to add scripts to WordPress site's and just. >

WP Reset – Best WordPress Reset Plugin

WordPress Reset resets any WordPress site to the default values without modifying any files. >

Advanced Automatic Updates

Adds extra options to WordPress' built-in Automatic Updates feature. >

Portfolio Post Type

This plugin registers a custom post type for portfolio items. >

CMS Tree Page View

Adds a tree view of all pages & custom posts. >

Reveal IDs

What this plugin does is to reveal most removed IDs on admin pages, as it. >

WordPress Database Reset

A plugin that allows you to skip the 5 minute installation and reset WordPress's database. >

Admin Columns

Customise columns on the administration screens for post(types), pages, media, comments, links and users with. >

Categories Images

The Categories Images Plugin allow you to add image with category or taxonomy. >

WP Robots Txt

WP Robots Txt Allows you to edit the content of your robots.txt file.
>

Disable XML-RPC

This plugin disables XML-RPC API in WordPress 3.5+, which is enabled by default. >

Disable XML-RPC Pingback

Stops abuse of your site's XML-RPC by simply removing some methods used by attackers. >

Simple History

View changes made by users within WordPress. See who created a page, uploaded an attachment. >

WP-Paginate

WP-Paginate is a simple and flexible pagination plugin which provides users with better navigation on. >

The WP Remote WordPress Plugin

WP Remote is a free web app that enables you to easily manage all of. >

Advanced Custom Fields: Font Awesome Field

Adds a new 'Font Awesome Icon' field to the popular Advanced Custom Fields plugin. >

Bulk Delete

Bulk delete posts, pages, users, attachments and meta fields based on different conditions and filters. >

WP Hide Post

Enables you to control the visibility of items on your blog by making posts/pages hidden. >

Activity Log

The #1 Activity Log plugin helps you monitor & log all changes and activities on. >

WP Crontrol

WP Crontrol lets you view and control what's happening in the WP-Cron system. >

Capability Manager Enhanced

A simple way to manage WordPress roles and capabilities. >

Customizer Export/Import

Easily export or import your WordPress customizer settings! >

What The File

What The File is the best tool to find out what template parts are used. >

WordPress REST API (Version 2)

Access your site's data through an easy-to-use HTTP REST API. (Version 2) >

SSH SFTP Updater Support

"SSH SFTP Updater Support" is the easiest way to keep your WordPress installation up-to-date with. >

AG Custom Admin

All-in-one tool for admin panel customization. >

WP Admin UI Customize

Customize the management screen UI. >

Custom Field Suite

Add custom fields to your post types. >

Ultimate Category Excluder

Ultimate Category Excluder allows you to quickly and easily exclude categories from your front page. >

Meta Tag Manager

Easily add and manage custom meta tags to various parts of your site or on. >

File Manager

File Manager provides you ability to edit, delete, upload, download, copy and paste files and. >

String locator

Find and edit code or texts in your themes and plugins. >

WP Mobile Menu

Need some help with the mobile website experience? Need an Mobile Menu plugin that keep. >

Remove Footer Credit

Remove or change footer credits or any text or HTML without modifying code. >

Calculated Fields Form

Calculated Fields Form is a plugin for creating forms with dynamically calculated fields and display. >

Absolutely Glamorous Custom Admin

With this plugin you can easily customize WordPress admin panel, login page, admin menu, admin. >

WP Rollback

Rollback (or forward) any WordPress.org plugin or theme like a boss. >

Show Current Template

A WordPress plugin which shows the current template file name, the current theme name and. >

Query Monitor

Query Monitor is the developer tools panel for WordPress. >

WordPress Infinite Scroll – Ajax Load More

The ultimate infinite scroll and lazy load solution for your WordPress powered website. >

Export WordPress data to XML/CSV

WP All Export is an extremely powerful exporter that makes it easy to export any. >

If Menu

Display or hide menu items with user-defines rules. >

Duplicate Menu

Easily duplicate your WordPress menus with one click. >

jQuery Updater

This plugin updates jQuery to the latest stable version on your website. >

Companion Auto Update

This plugin automatically updates all plugins, all themes and the wordpress core in the background. >

Media File Renamer

Automatically rename files depending on Media titles dynamically + update links. Pro version has many. >

My Custom Functions

Easily and safely add your custom PHP code to your WordPress website, directly out of. >

Htaccess Editor

A safe & simple htaccess file editor with automatic backup. >

PHP Settings

This plugin provides a simple user interface with a code editor to edit your local. >

Debug Bar

Adds a debug menu to the admin bar that shows query, cache, and other helpful. >

Site Optimization & Performance Plugins (12)

WP-Optimize

WP-Optimize is WordPress's most-installed optimization plugin. With it, you can clean up your database easily. >

Smush Image Compression and Optimization

Compress and optimize (or optimise) image files, improve performance and boost your SEO rank using >

Autoptimize

Autoptimize speeds up your website by optimizing JS, CSS, HTML, Google Fonts and images, async-ing. >

AMP for WP – Accelerated Mobile Pages

AMP for WP is the most recommended AMP plugin by the community. Automatically add Accelerated. >

Compress JPEG & PNG images

Speed up your website. Optimize your JPEG and PNG images automatically with TinyPNG. >

ShortPixel Image Optimizer

Speed up your website and boost your SEO by compressing old & new images. >

BJ Lazy Load

Lazy loading for images and iframes makes your site load faster and saves bandwidth. >

Lazy Load

Lazy load images to improve page load times and server bandwidth. >

Remove Query Strings From Static Resources

Remove query strings from static resources like CSS & JS files. >

a3 Lazy Load

Use a3 Lazy Load for images, videos, iframes. Instantly improve your sites load time. >

Clearfy – WordPress optimization plugin and disable ultimate tweaker

Optimize and tweak WordPress by disable unused features. Improve performance, SEO and security using Clearfy. >

Fast Velocity Minify

Improve your speed score on GTmetrix, Pingdom Tools and Google PageSpeed Insights by merging and. >

Async JavaScript

Async Javascript lets you add 'async' or 'defer' attribute to scripts to exclude to help. >

WP Performance Score Booster

Speed-up page load times and improve website scores in services like PageSpeed, YSlow, Pingdom and. >

Hummingbird Page Speed Optimization

Make your site load faster with file compression, minification and a complete set of cache. >

Optimize Database after Deleting Revisions

This plugin is a 'One Click' WordPress Database Cleaner / Optimizer. >

Adminimize

Adminimize that lets you hide 'unnecessary' items from the WordPress backend. >

Site Unavailable/Maintenance Plugins (4)

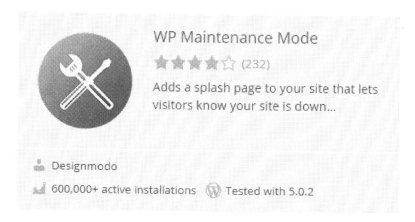

WP Maintenance Mode

Adds a splash page to your site that lets visitors know your site is down. >

Maintenance

Maintenance – easy configure and customize coming soon, under construction page when site have updates. >

Coming Soon Page & Maintenance Mode by SeedProd

The #1 Coming Soon Page, Under Construction & Maintenance Mode plugin for WordPress. >

Under Construction / Maintenance Mode from Acurax

The easiest and feature-rich plugin to show under construction, coming soon, maintenance mode to visitors. >

Sitemap Plugins (7)

Google XML Sitemaps

★★★★★ (2,001)

This plugin will improve SEO by helping search enginess better index your site using sitemaps.

Arne Brachhold

2+ million active installations Tested with 5.0.2

Google XML Sitemaps

This plugin will improve SEO by helping search enginess better index your site using sitemaps. >

WP Sitemap Page

Add a sitemap on any of your page using the simple shortcode [wp_sitemap_page]. >

XML Sitemap & Google News

XML and Google News Sitemaps to feed the hungry spiders. Multisite, WP Super Cache, and Polylang. >

Google Sitemap by BestWebSoft

Generate and add XML sitemap to WordPress website. Help search engines index your blog. >

Simple Sitemap

The best HTML5 sitemap available for WordPress! No setup required. Flexible customization options available. >

Sitemap

[pagelist], [subpages], [siblings] and [pagelist_ext] shortcodes >

Simple Wp Sitemap

An easy sitemap plugin that adds both an xml and an html sitemap to your. >

Slider Plugins (12)

MetaSlider

Easy to use WordPress slider plugin. Create SEO-optimized responsive slideshows with Nivo Slider, Flex Slider. >

Master Slider – Responsive Touch Slider

Build SEO friendly sliders fast and easy with Master Slider. The most advanced responsive HTML5. >

Slider by Soliloquy – Responsive Image Slider for WordPress

The best WordPress slider plugin. Drag & Drop responsive slider builder that helps you create. >

Easing Slider

The easiest way to create sliders with WordPress. >

Smart Slider 3

Responsive slider plugin to create sliders in visual editor easily. Build beautiful image slider, layer. >

Meteor Slides

Easily create responsive slideshows with WordPress that are mobile friendly and simple to customize. >

Slider by 10Web – Responsive Image Slider

Slider by 10Web plugin is the perfect slider solution for WordPress. >

Slide Anything – Responsive Content / HTML Slider and Carousel

Create responsive carousels or sliders where the content for each slide can be anything you. >

Ultimate Responsive Image Slider Plugin

Ultimate responsive image slider plugin is by far the most advanced and responsive image slider. >

Slider by Nivo – Responsive WordPress Image Slider

Nivo Slider is The Most Popular And Easiest to Use Responsive WordPress Slider Plugin. >

Crelly Slider

A free responsive slider that supports layers. Add texts, images, videos and beautify them with. >

Ultimate Responsive Image Slider

Add Fully Responsive Image Slider To Your WordPress Blog. >

Social Media & Sharing Plugins (42)

AddToAny Share Buttons

Share buttons for WordPress including the AddToAny sharing button, Facebook, Twitter, Google+, Pinterest, WhatsApp, many. >

Instagram Feed

Display beautifully clean, customizable, and responsive feeds from multiple Instagram accounts. >

Simple Social Icons

This plugin allows you to insert social icons in any widget area. >

Social Share Icons & Social Share Buttons

Social sharing plugin adding social buttons. >

WordPress Share Buttons Plugin – AddThis

Share buttons from AddThis help you get more traffic from sharing through social networks. >

Custom Facebook Feed

The Custom Facebook Feed allows you to display completely customizable Facebook feeds of any public. >

NextScripts: Social Networks Auto-Poster

Automatically publishes blogposts to profiles/pages/groups on Facebook, Twitter, Instagram, and more. >

Free Tools to Automate Your Site Growth

Free and easy way to double your email subscribers, plus sharing tools to double your traffic. >

WP Instagram Widget

WP Instagram widget is a no fuss WordPress widget to showcase your latest Instagram pics. >

Simple Share Buttons Adder

A simple plugin that enables you to add share buttons to all of your posts. >

WordPress Share Buttons, Related Posts, Google Analytics – Shareaholic

Improve Audience Engagement with Award Winning Site-Speed Optimized Social Tools. >

Easy Facebook Like Box (Facebook Page Plugin)

Easy Facebook like box WordPress plugin allows to display custom Facebook feed, page plugin. >

Facebook Widget

This widget adds a Simple Facebook page Like Widget into your WordPress website Sidebar. >

Instagram Slider Widget

Instagram Slider Widget is a responsive slider widget that shows 12 latest images from a. >

Social Media and Share Icons (Ultimate Social Media)

Easy to use social media plugin which adds social media icons to your website with. >

WP to Twitter

Posts a Twitter update when you update your WordPress blog or add a link. >

10Web Instagram Feed – Instagram Gallery

10Web Instagram Feed is a user-friendly plugin to display user or hashtag-based Instagram feeds. >

Facebook

Facebook Like Box plugin comes with Facebook Like Box Widget & Shortcode. >

Tracking Code Manager

A plugin to manage ALL your tracking code and conversion pixels. >

Feed Them Social – Facebook, Instagram, Twitter, YouTube & Pinterest

Custom feeds for Facebook Pages, Album Photos, Videos & Covers, Instagram, Twitter, Pinterest & YouTube. >

PixelYourSite – Facebook Pixel (Events, WooCommerce & Easy Digital Downloads)

Insert the new Facebook Pixel on WordPress, add Events, enjoy superb WooCommerce & EDD Facebook. >

Social Share Buttons – Social Pug

The best social sharing plugin for your WordPress website and the only social sharing plugin >

Pinterest Pin It Button On Image Hover And Post

Pin Your WordPress Blog Posts Pages Images With Pinterest Plugin. >

WP Facebook Auto Publish

Publish posts automatically to Facebook page or profile. >

I Recommend This

This plugin allows your visitors to simply like/recommend your posts instead of comment on it. >

Better Click To Tweet

Insert click to tweet boxes into your posts, simply and securely. Gutenberg/WordPress 5.X+ block included. >

Table Plugins (10)

TablePress

★★★★★ (3,369)

Embed beautiful and feature-rich tables into your posts and pages, without having to write code.

Tobias Bäthge

700,000+ active installations Tested with 5.0.2

TablePress

Embed beautiful and feature-rich tables into your posts and pages, without having to write code. >

Easy Table

Easy Table is WordPress plugin to create table in post, page, or widget in easy. >

Easy Table of Contents

Adds a user friendly and fully automatic way to create and display a table of. >

Visualizer: Tables and Charts Manager for WordPress (Lite)

A simple and quite powerful WordPress chart plugin to create and embed interactive charts. >

Pricing Tables WordPress Plugin – Easy Pricing Tables

Pricing Table Plugin – Easy Pricing Tables Lets You Create A Beautiful, Responsive Pricing Table. >

Pricing Table by Supsystic

Pricing Table generator by Supsystic allows you to create responsive pricing tables or comparison table. >

Data Tables Generator by Supsystic

Create data tables with charts and graphs. WooCommerce Integration. >

Responsive Pricing Table

A responsive and elegant way to present your offer to your visitors. >

Advanced Custom Fields: Table Field

A Table Field Add-on for the Advanced Custom Fields Plugin. >

Ninja Tables – WP Data Tables Plugin for WordPress

No.1 Table Plugin for WordPress with beautiful, fast and amazing responsive table features and fully. >

User Management Plugins (15)

Advanced Access Manager

All you need to manage access to you WordPress websites on frontend, backend and API. >

User Role Editor

User Role Editor WordPress plugin makes user roles and capabilities changing easy. Edit/add/delete WordPress user. >

WP User Avatar

Use any image from your WordPress Media Library as a custom user avatar. >

Nav Menu Roles

Hide custom menu items based on user roles. >

WP-UserOnline

Enable you to display how many users are online on your WordPress blog with detailed. >

Simple Local Avatars

Adds an avatar upload field to user profiles. Generates requested sizes on demand just like. >

User Switching

Instant switching between user accounts in WordPress. >

Edit Author Slug

Allows an admin (or capable user) to edit the author slug of a user, and. >

WPFront User Role Editor

Easily allows you to manage WordPress user roles. You can create, edit, delete and manage. >

User registration & user profile – Profile Builder

Simple to use profile plugin allowing front-end login, user registration and edit profile by using. >

User Access Manager

With the "User Access Manager"-plugin you can manage the access to your posts, pages and. >

Remove Dashboard Access

Allows you to disable Dashboard access for users of a specific role or capability. >

Simple Author Box

Adds a cool responsive author box with social icons on your posts. >

User Profile Picture

Set a custom profile image (avatar) for a user using the standard WordPress media upload. >

Import users from CSV with meta

A plugin to import users using CSV files to WP database automatically including custom user. >

Widget & Sidebar Plugins (27)

Widget Importer & Exporter

Import and export your widgets. >

Custom Sidebars – Dynamic Widget Area Manager

Flexible sidebars for custom widget configurations on every page, post and custom post type. >

SiteOrigin Widgets Bundle

The SiteOrigin widget bundle gives you a collection of widgets that you can use and. >

Widget Logic

Widget Logic lets you control on which pages widgets appear using WP's conditional tags. >

Image Widget

Image Widget is a simple plugin that uses the native WordPress media manager to add image widgets to your site. >

Widget Options

Get Better Control over your Widgets. Easily show or hide WordPress widgets on specified pages. >

WP Page Widget

Select widgets for each page / post / custom post type. For every single page. >

Contact Widgets

Beautifully display social media and contact information on your website with these simple widgets. >

WooSidebars

WooSidebars adds functionality to display different widgets in a sidebar. >

Q2W3 Fixed Widget

Fixes positioning of the selected widgets, when the page is scrolled down. >

Widget CSS Classes

Add custom classes and ids plus first, last, even, odd, and numbered classes to your site. >

WP Tab Widget

WP Tab Widget is the AJAXified plugin which loads content by demand, and thus it. >

Category Posts Widget

Adds a widget that shows the most recent posts from a single category. >

Dynamic Widgets

Dynamic Widgets gives you full control on which pages a widget will display. >

Simple Image Widget

A simple widget that makes it a breeze to add images to your sidebars. >

amr shortcode any widget

Insert a widget or multiple widgets or a entire widget area (sidebar) into a page. >

Widgets on Pages

The easiest and highest rated way to Add Widgets or Sidebars to Posts and Pages. >

Enhanced Text Widget

An enhanced version of the text widget that supports Text, HTML, CSS, JavaScript, Flash, Shortcodes. >

Widget Context

Show or hide widgets on specific posts, pages or sections of your site. >

Simple Page Sidebars

Easily assign custom, widget-enabled sidebars to any page. >

Widget Shortcode

Adds [widget] shortcode which enables you to output widgets anywhere you like. >

Content Blocks (Custom Post Widget)

This plugin enables you to edit and display Content Blocks in a sidebar widget. >

Content Aware Sidebars – Unlimited Widget Areas

Display widget areas and custom sidebars on any post, page, category etc. Supports bbPress, BuddyPress, >

Livemesh SiteOrigin Widgets

A collection of premium quality widgets for use in any widgetized area or in SiteOrigin. >

Widgets for SiteOrigin

A collection of highly customizable and thoughtfully crafted widgets. Built on top of the SiteOrigin. >

Widget Content Blocks

Edit widget content using the default WordPress visual editor and media uploading functionality. >

T(-) Countdown

T(-) Countdown will display a highly customizable, HTML5 countdown timer as a sidebar widget. >

WooCommerce Plugins (30)

WooCommerce

WooCommerce is a powerful, extendable eCommerce plugin that helps you sell anything. Beautifully. >

WooCommerce Stripe Payment Gateway

Take credit card payments on your store using Stripe. >

YITH WooCommerce Compare

YITH WooCommerce Compare allows you to compare more products of your shop in one complete. >

YITH WooCommerce Ajax Product Filter

YITH WooCommerce Ajax Product Filter offers you the perfect way to filter all products of. >

WordPress Download Manager

WordPress Download Manager is a Files / Documents Management Plugin to manage, track and control. >

WooCommerce PDF Invoices & Packing Slips

Create, print & automatically email PDF invoices & packing slips for WooCommerce orders. >

YITH WooCommerce Quick View

This plugin adds the possibility to have a quick preview of the products right from. >

WooCommerce Grid / List toggle

Adds a grid/list view toggle to product archives. >

WooCommerce Customizer

Helps you customize WooCommerce without writing any code! >

WooCommerce Menu Cart

Automatically displays a shopping cart in your menu bar. >

WooCommerce Print Invoice & Delivery Note

Print invoices and delivery notes for WooCommerce orders. >

WooCommerce PagSeguro

Adds PagSeguro gateway to the WooCommerce plugin. >

Booster for WooCommerce

Supercharge your WordPress WooCommerce site with these awesome powerful features. >

Checkout Field Editor (Checkout Manager) for WooCommerce

Checkout Field Editor (Checkout Manager) for WooCommerce. >

WOOF – Products Filter for WooCommerce

WooCommerce Products Filter – flexible, easy and robust professional filter for products in the WooCommerce. >

WordPress Simple PayPal Shopping Cart

Very easy to use Simple WordPress PayPal Shopping Cart Plugin. Great for selling products online. >

WooCommerce Print Invoice & Delivery Notes

Print invoices and delivery notes for WooCommerce orders. >

Custom Product Tabs for WooCommerce

Add custom tabs with content to products in WooCommerce. >

Advanced Order Export For WooCommerce

Export orders from WooCommerce with ease. >

PayPal for WooCommerce

One plugin for all things PayPal! Express Checkout with Smart Payment Buttons, PayPal Pro, Braintree. >

WooCommerce Germanized

Extends WooCommerce to become a legally compliant Shop for German Market. Must Have for every. >

WooCommerce Correios

Integration between the Correios and WooCommerce. >

Product Import Export for WooCommerce

Easily import products into WooCommerce store or export WooCommerce products from the store. Import WooCommerce. >

Mollie Payments for WooCommerce

Accept all major payment methods in WooCommerce today. Credit cards, iDEAL, bitcoin and more! Fast. >

Variation Swatches for WooCommerce

An extension of WooCommerce that make variable products be more beauty and friendly to customers. >

WooCommerce Variation Swatches

Beautiful Color, Image and Buttons Variation Swatches For WooCommerce Product. >

WooCommerce Extra Checkout Fields for Brazil

Adds Brazilian checkout fields in WooCommerce. >

WooCommerce Advanced Free Shipping

WooCommerce Advanced Free Shipping is an plugin which allows you to set up advanced free. >

WooCommerce Cart Tab

Adds an offscreen cart to all pages on your site and a fixed tab that. >

Enhanced Ecommerce Google Analytics Plugin for WooCommerce

Provides integration between Enhanced Ecommerce feature of Google Analytics and WooCommerce. >

WooCommerce Products Per Page

WooCommerce Products Per Page is a easy-to-setup plugin that integrates a 'products per page' dropdown. >

WooCommerce Wishlist Plugin

Allow your store guests and customers to add products to Wishlist. Add Wishlist functionality to. >

Advanced Woo Search

Advanced AJAX search plugin for WooCommerce. >

WooCommerce Weight Based Shipping

Simple yet flexible weight-based shipping for WooCommerce. >

Flexible Shipping for WooCommerce

The most flexible Table Rate Shipping WooCommerce plugin. Create virtually any shipping scenario you need. >

AfterShip – WooCommerce Tracking

Auto import tracking of all your shipments in one place to WooCommerce (Free), branded tracking. >

WooCommerce Extended Coupon Features FREE

Additional functionality for WooCommerce Coupons: Allow discounts to be automatically applied, applying coupons via. >

WooCommerce PDF Invoices

Automatically generate and attach customizable PDF Invoices and PDF Packing Slips for WooCommerce emails and. >

Ajax Search for WooCommerce

Help users easily find and discover products in your store using Ajax Search for WooCommerce. >

YouTube & Video Plugins (8)

YouTube

YouTube Embed WordPress Plugin. Embed a responsive video, YouTube channel gallery, playlist gallery, or YouTube.com. >

Advanced Responsive Video Embedder

Easy responsive video embeds via URLs or shortcodes. Perfect drop-in replacement for WordPress' default embeds. >

YouTube Embed

An incredibly fast, simple, yet powerful, method of embedding YouTube videos into your WordPress site. >

YouTube Widget Responsive

Share your channel with YouTube button subscribe. >

WP Video Lightbox

Very easy to use WordPress lightbox plugin to display YouTube and Vimeo videos in an. >

ARVE Advanced Responsive Video Embedder

Easy responsive video embeds via URLs or shortcodes. Perfect drop-in replacement for WordPress' default embeds. >

FV Flowplayer Video Player

WordPress's most reliable, easy to use and feature-rich video player. Supports responsive design, HTML5, playlists. >

Video Embed & Thumbnail Generator

Makes video thumbnails, allows resolution switching, and embeds responsive self-hosted videos and galleries. >

Please take a few seconds to leave a review on Amazon. Your thoughts are appreciated!

www.digitalfodder.com

Up to 87% off WordPress Hosting

https://www.digitalfodder.com/cheap-web-hosting-for-wordpress/

Up to 20% off Elegant Themes

https://www.digitalfodder.com/elegant-themes-coupon-discount/

Made in the USA
Lexington, KY
28 May 2019